The 2012-2013 San Francisco 49ers:

The NFC Championship, The Kaepernick - Smith Controversy, & the Road to the NFL 2013 Super Bowl

Dan Fathow

Megalodon Entertainment, LLC.

Published by Megalodon Entertainment, LLC. (USA)
www.MegalodonEntertainment.com

First Printing: January 2013

Copyright © 2013 Megalodon Entertainment LLC. All rights reserved.

All rights reserved under the International and Pan-American Copyright conventions. No part of this publication may be reproduced, or transmitted by any means in any form (electronic, photocopying, mechanical, recording, or any other method), without the specific written permission of the publisher. Please, direct questions to info@megalodonentertainment.com.

Printed in the United States of America.

ISBN: 978-1-61589-040-8
ISBN-10: 1-61589-040-8

The NFL, National Football League, San Francisco 49ers, Super Bowl, AFC, NFC, and all team names, locations, and events are ™ of their respective owners. No affiliation to any teams, players, or intellectual properties is claimed or implied by this publication.

BULK INQUERIES:

Quantity discounts are available on bulk orders of this novel for educational, fund-raising, promotional, and special sales purposes. For details, please contact www.MegalodonEntertainment.com

Check Out Another Great Book from Megalodon Entertainment LLC

From Lewis Aleman, Bestselling Author of Cold Streak & Faces in Time

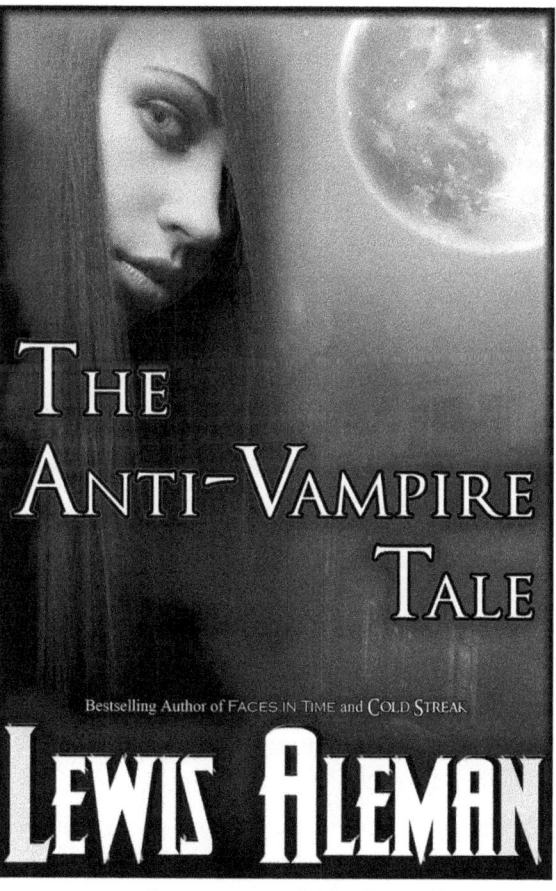

Simon is a vampire, prowling through the dark New Orleans streets that pulse with wild adventure and fangs gleaming in the shadows. He's spent the last few decades as a recluse, aching over a lost love. Now, he's put it behind him, thirsting to fulfill the raging inner need he's deprived himself for so long.

Ruby feels isolated and out of place--lonely, shy, but too strong-minded to go along with the crowd. All that changes when she is dragged out for her birthday and ends up dancing with Simon--mysterious, blue-eyed, and gorgeous. Her body tingles watching his muscled form move--so fast, so smooth, so powerful. His smile is otherworldly, and his kiss charges her with electric energy. All seems to be going well until three other vampires appear in the crowd, turning the dance floor into a horror show.

Real Vampires...Don't Sparkle

www.LewisAleman.com
Facebook.com/LewisAleman
Youtube.com/LewisAleman

Check out more Great Releases from Megalodon Entertainment LLC

The Next Book in the Saga...

PRAISE FOR LEWIS ALEMAN:

"There is craftsmanship in Aleman's details; elaborate use of adjectival simile and metaphor ... stimulates ... memorable ... space-time research well done"
Dionne Charlet
Where Y'At Magazine
Feb 2010

"*Faces in Time* was an adventurous, fast paced, time traveling novel...loved the twists and turns...Lewis writes beautifully, his work is filled with great detailed descriptions...a great adventure. I haven't seen anything out like it."
La Femme Readers
December 12, 2009

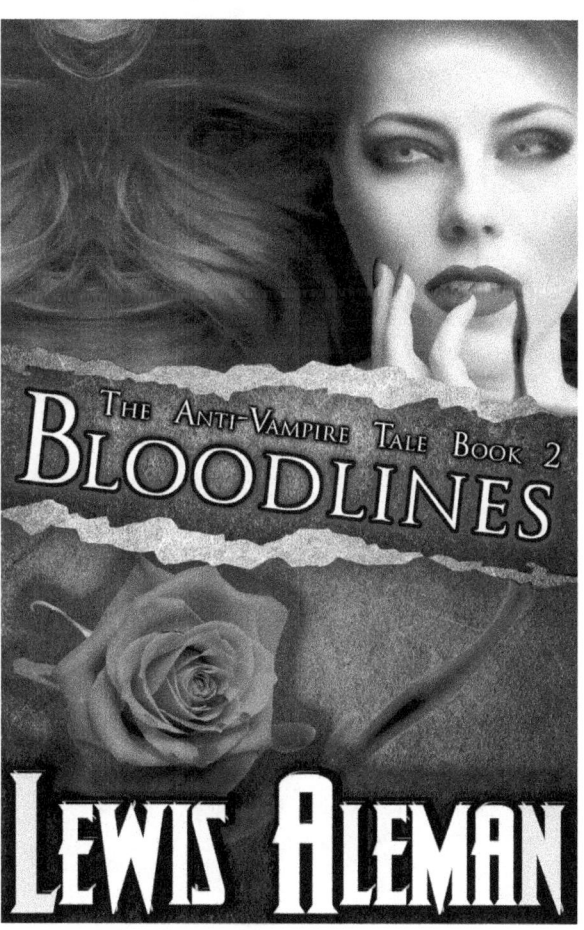

ISBN-13: 978-1-61589-028-6
ISBN: 1-61589-028-9

WWW.LEWISALEMAN.COM
FACEBOOK.COM/LEWISALEMAN
YOUTUBE.COM/LEWISALEMAN

THE 2012-2013 SAN FRANCISCO 49ERS:

THE NFC CHAMPIONSHIP, THE KAEPERNICK - SMITH CONTROVERSY, & THE ROAD TO THE NFL 2013 SUPER BOWL

Dan Fathow

MEGALODON ENTERTAINMENT, LLC.

TABLE OF CONTENTS

PART I: 2012 NFC CHAMPIONSHIP SEASON

Week 1 vs. Green Bay Packers 13

Week 2 vs. Detroit Lions 17

Week 3 vs. Minnesota Vikings 21

Week 4 vs. New York Jets....................... 24

Week 5 vs. Buffalo Bills 29

Week 6 vs. New York Giants 33

Week 7 vs. Seattle Seahawks 37

Week 8 vs. Arizona Cardinals 41

Week 9 (Bye Week – no content)

Week 10 vs. St. Louis Rams 45

Week 11 vs. Chicago Bears 49

Week 12 vs. New Orleans Saints................ 53

Week 13 vs. St. Louis Rams 59

Week 14 vs. Miami Dolphins..................... 64

Week 15 vs. New England Patriots 68

Week 16 vs. Seattle Seahawks 72

Week 17 vs. Arizona Cardinals 76

Week 18 vs. Green Bay Packers 80

Week 19 vs. Atlanta Falcons 85

PART II: THE SMITH – KAEPERNICK QUARTERBACK
	CONTROVERSY **93**

PART III: SUPER BOWL XLVII
	THE MATCHUP VS. THE RAVENS . **98**

PART IV: THE QUARTERBACK MATCHUP
	FLACCO VS KAEPERNICK **101**

Part I:
The Magnificent Season

2012 – 2013 SAN FRANCISCO 49ERS 13

WEEK 1

September 9, 2012
Lambeau Field – Green Bay, WI

Teams	1st	2nd	3rd	4th	Total
Green Bay Packers	0	7	0	15	**22**
San Francisco 49ers	3	13	7	7	**30**

GAME SUMMARY

The opening game of the San Francisco 49ers' 2012 season had them facing the daunting task of playing the Green Bay Packers at home.

As in recent years, the Packers were considered serious Super Bowl contenders, and no one predicted they would lose the season opener at home.

While only throwing for 211 yards, Alex Smith had a great day slinging 2 touchdowns into the end zone with 0 interceptions. Those statistics are even more impressive when one takes into account that Smith was sacked 4 times in this contest.

By comparison, Aaron Rodgers threw for 303 yards, but he only matched Smith on TD passes with 2. The big difference in the performances of these 2 quarterbacks was that Smith kept the ball in his team's hands while Rodgers threw an interception.

One telling fact was that the 49ers defense held Green Bay to only 45 yards, with Aaron Rodgers being the leading rusher for the Packers with only 27 yards.

Conversely, the 49ers had a great day on the ground, running for 186 yards. The leading rusher was Frank Gore, who went for 112 yards and 1 touchdown. The next highest rusher was Kendall Hunter for 41 yards on 9 carries.

Kicker David Akers was perfect in this contest, counting for 12 points on 3 of 3 field goals and 3 of 3 extra points.

Beating Green Bay at home was an excellent way for the 49ers to start the season and demonstrate that they were a championship caliber team and a serious Super Bowl threat.

Team Leaders

Passing

Alex Smith #11
211 Yards, 2 Touchdowns, 0 Interceptions
(20/26, 76.92 Comp %)

Rushing

Frank Gore #21
112 Yards on 16 Carries
7.00 Yards per Carry
1 Rushing Touchdown

Kendall Hunter #32
41 Yards on 9 Carries
4.56 Yards per Carry
0 Rushing Touchdowns

2012 – 2013 San Francisco 49ers 15

Colin Kaepernick #7
17 Yards on 1 Carry
17 Yards per Carry
0 Rushing Touchdowns

Receiving

Michael Crabtree #15
76 Yards on 7 Receptions
10.86 Yards per Reception
0 Touchdown Receptions

Randy Moss #84
47 Yards on 4 Receptions
11.75 Yards per Reception
1 Touchdown Reception

Vernon Davis #85
43 Yards on 3 Receptions
14.33 Yards per Reception
1 Touchdown Reception

Mario Manningham #82
29 Yards on 4 Receptions
7.25 Yards per Reception
0 Touchdown Receptions

Kicking

David Akers #2
12 Points Total
3/3 Field Goals
3/3 Extra Points

Dan Fathow 16

Interceptions

Navorro Bowman #53
1 Interception

THE BOTTOM LINE

1 - 0

WEEK 2

September 16, 2012
Candlestick Park – San Francisco, CA

Teams	1st	2nd	3rd	4th	Total
Detroit Lions	6	0	3	10	**19**
San Francisco 49ers	7	7	3	10	**27**

GAME SUMMARY

After an impressive road win over Green Bay, the San Francisco 49ers were back at home, facing the Detroit Lions.

Coming into this game the Lions were 1-0, having won their season opener at home.

Alex Smith had a good game, passing for 226 yards and 2 touchdowns with 0 interceptions, while being sacked 3 times. His counterpart, Matthew Stafford had a similar game throwing for 230 yards; however, he had 1 less touchdown and 1 interception. Smith clearly had the superior performance.

The 49ers won total yards 349 to 296. While keeping the Lions to only 82 rushing yards, San Francisco was able to rack up 148 yards on the ground.

In the air, Vernon Davis had a great day, catching 5 balls for 73 yards, 2 of those being touchdown receptions. Michael Crabtree also caught 6 passes for 67 yards.

Dan Fathow 18

Team Leaders

Passing

Alex Smith #11
226 Yards, 2 Touchdowns, 0 Interceptions
(20/31, 64.52 Comp %)

Rushing

Frank Gore #21
89 Yards on 17 Carries
5.24 Yards per Carry
1 Rushing Touchdown

Mario Manningham #82
29 Yards on 1 Carry
29.00 Yards per Carry
0 Rushing Touchdowns

Receiving

Vernon Davis #85
73 Yards on 5 Receptions
14.60 Yards per Reception
2 Touchdown Receptions

2012 – 2013 San Francisco 49ers 19

Michael Crabtree #15
67 Yards on 6 Receptions
11.17 Yards per Reception
0 Touchdown Receptions

Mario Manningham #82
28 Yards on 3 Receptions
9.33 Yards per Reception
0 Touchdown Receptions

Kendall Hunter #32
21 Yards on 2 Receptions
10.5 Yards per Reception
0 Touchdown Reception

Kicking

David Akers #2
9 Points Total
2/2 Field Goals
3/3 Extra Points

Interceptions

Dashon Goldson #38
1 Interception

Dan Fathow 20
The Bottom Line
2 - 0

WEEK 3

September 23, 2012
Mall of America Field – Minneapolis, MN

Teams	1st	2nd	3rd	4th	**Total**
Minnesota Vikings	7	10	0	7	**24**
San Francisco 49ers	0	3	10	0	**13**

GAME SUMMARY

Week 3 had the 49ers on the road again, this time in Minneapolis to face the Vikings. At this point, San Francisco had a record of 2-0, including their impressive victory over Green Bay, and the Vikings were 1-1. Surely not many people were predicting an 11-point loss for the 49ers.

Alex Smith had a mixed day, throwing for only 204 yards with 1 touchdown and 1 interception. He was sacked 3 times in this game, which may have contributed to his first interception of the season. Smith was also the second highest rusher for the 49ers in this game with 26 yards of his own on 4 carries.

San Francisco lost the turnover war 3-2, which usually spells doom in the NFL.

One of the key differences in this game was in the ground attack. The 49ers, who previously had rushed for 186 and 148 yards, were held to only 89 yards in this contest. On the other side, the Vikings rushed for 146 yards, mostly due to Adrian Peterson putting up 86 yards on 25 carries. Opposing quarterback Christian Ponder also rushed for 33 yards on 7 runs.

Team Leaders

Passing

Alex Smith #11
204 Yards, 1 Touchdown, 1 Interception
(24/35, 68.57 Comp %)

Rushing

Frank Gore #21
63 Yards on 12 Carries
5.25 Yards per Carry
0 Rushing Touchdowns

Alex Smith #11
26 Yards on 4 Carry
6.50 Yards per Carry
0 Rushing Touchdowns

Receiving

Mario Manningham #82
56 Yards on 5 Receptions
11.20 Yards per Reception
0 Touchdown Receptions

2012 – 2013 SAN FRANCISCO 49ERS 23

Vernon Davis #85
53 Yards on 5 Receptions
10.60 Yards per Reception
1 Touchdown Reception

Michael Crabtree #15
40 Yards on 6 Receptions
6.67 Yards per Reception
0 Touchdown Receptions

Randy Moss #84
27 Yards on 3 Receptions
9.00 Yards per Reception
0 Touchdown Receptions

Kicking

David Akers #2
7 Points Total
2/3 Field Goals
1/1 Extra Points

Interceptions

None

THE BOTTOM LINE

2 - 1

WEEK 4

September 30, 2012
MetLife Stadium – East Rutherford, NJ

Teams	1st	2nd	3rd	4th	Total
New York Jets	0	0	0	0	**0**
San Francisco 49ers	0	10	7	17	**34**

GAME SUMMARY

So, 2012 proved to be a disastrous year for the New York Jets. They had an infamous quarterback debacle in which starter Mark Sanchez was grossly underperforming, and then there was the mindboggling refusal to utilize Tim Tebow *after* trading to get him. There was enough going on with Jets management, coaches, and players in 2012 for an entire book of its own.

Both new and long-term 49ers fans can understand the weight and impact of a controversial quarterback situation. There was the legendary Joe Montana and Steve Young controversy in the early 90s, and in this very season, there would be another between Alex Smith and Colin Kaepernick.

However, for the purposes of this discussion, it's merely important to point out that the Jets were performing *MUCH* better in Game 3 than they were at the end of the year. By year's end, the Jets would be 6-10 with nearly twice as many losses as wins, but back in Week 4 coming into the home game versus the 49ers, the Jets were 2-1 and actually had twice as many wins as losses. So, the Jets were performing better and were considered to be a better team in the early part of the season.

The 49ers' 34-0 shutout-devastation that ensued in this game was not expected. Two weeks after this defeat, the Jets soundly beat the Indianapolis Colts 35-9, and the next week they barely lost to the New England Patriots 29-26 in overtime. Both of those teams made it to the playoffs. The Jets were still a competitive team at this point in time; the 49ers just seriously outplayed them.

In this contest, the 49ers defense held Mark Sanchez to an anemic 103 yards on 13 of 29 pass attempts with 0 touchdowns and 1 interception. Tim Tebow threw for only 1 pass which was completed for 9 yards.

In addition to crushing the Jets air attempts, the 49ers also put a clamp on their rushing game, holding them to only 45 total rushing yards. The top rusher for the Jets was Shonn Greene, who only had 34 yards on 11 carriers.

Besides having a great defensive outing, San Francisco also had a strong offensive day, putting up 381 total yards, 134 in the air and 247 on the ground. The ground game differential was really what made the difference in this game, as the 49ers rushed for 202 more yards than their opponent.

Alex Smith threw for 134 yards on 12 of 21 passes for a 57.14 completion percentage with 0 touchdowns and 0 interceptions. While one might be quick to criticize Smith's low passing yardage and no passing touchdowns in this game, it is relevant to point out that the ground game was running all over the Jets. Why put the ball in the air and risk interception when your ground game and defense are shutting out your opponent 34-0?

Backup and future starter Colin Kaepernick was on the field in this contest, although he only threw 1 incomplete pass. He was much more effective running the ball as noted below.

The 49ers had 3 players rushing for 50 yards or more in this game: Frank Gore at 64 yards, Kendall Hunter at 56, and

Colin Kaepernick at 50. Each of these 3 players scored a rushing touchdown. Mario Manningham also had 1 long, breakaway run of 28 yards.

While it wasn't the biggest passing day for the 49ers, Mario Manningham had 3 receptions for 47 yards, followed by Delanie Walker with 31 yards on 2 passes.

Another key factor in this game was the turnover battle of which the 49ers clearly won 4-0. The beleaguered Jets had 3 lost fumbles and 1 interception. The lone interception was nabbed by Patrick Willis.

On the kicking front, David Akers had a mixed day hitting 2 of 4 field goals and 4 of 4 extra points, putting 10 points of his own through the uprights.

It was an impressive, dominating win for the 49ers that served as a bit of vindication after the previous week's loss to the Vikings.

TEAM LEADERS

Passing

Alex Smith #11
143 Yards, 0 Touchdowns, 0 Interceptions
(12/21, Comp 57.14 %)

Colin Kaepernick #7
0 Yards, 0 Touchdowns, 0 Interceptions
(0/1, Comp 00.00 %)

2012 – 2013 San Francisco 49ers 27

Rushing

Frank Gore #21
64 Yards on 20 Carries
3.20 Yards per Carry
1 Rushing Touchdown

Kendall Hunter #32
56 Yards on 8 Carries
7.00 Yards per Carry
1 Rushing Touchdown

Colin Kaepernick #7
50 Yards on 5 Carries
10.00 Yards per Carry
1 Rushing Touchdown

Mario Manningham #82
28 Yards on 1 Carry
28.00 Yards per Carry
1 Rushing Touchdown

Receiving

Mario Manningham #82
47 Yards on 3 Receptions
15.67 Yards per Reception
0 Touchdown Receptions

Delanie Walker #46
31 Yards on 2 Receptions
15.50 Yards per Reception
0 Touchdown Receptions

Dan Fathow 28

Vernon Davis #85
28 Yards on 2 Receptions
14.00 Yards per Reception
0 Touchdown Receptions

Michael Crabtree #15
15 Yards on 2 Receptions
7.50 Yards per Reception
0 Touchdown Receptions

Kicking

David Akers #2
10 Points Total
2/4 Field Goals
5/4 Extra Points

Interceptions

Patrick Willis #52
1 Interception

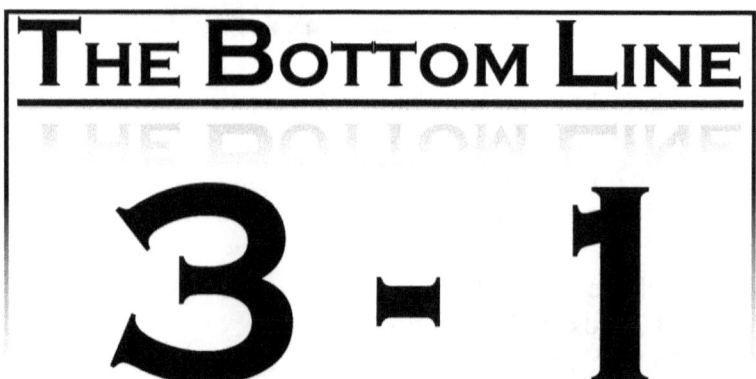

THE BOTTOM LINE

3 - 1

WEEK 5

October 7, 2012
Candlestick Park – San Francisco, CA

Teams	1st	2nd	3rd	4th	Total
Kansas City Chiefs	0	3	0	0	3
Baltimore Ravens	3	14	7	21	45

GAME SUMMARY

Week 5 was the second week in a row in which the 49ers completely blew out an opponent. This 42-point victory was a powerful performance in which San Francisco was firing on all cylinders.

Alex Smith had a fantastic game, racking up 303 yards with 3 touchdowns and 0 interceptions. He connected on 18 of 24 pass attempts for an impressive completion ratio of 75.00%.

Colin Kaepernick was once again in the game for 1 passing play, going 1 for 1 for 7 yards. His contributions for the second week in a row came in the form of rushing as documented below.

On the ground, the 49ers put up an impressive 311 yards. Leading rusher Frank Gore rushed for 106 yards and 1 touchdown, followed by Kendall Hunter who rushed on 11 carries for 81 yards. Alex Smith actually rushed for more yards than Colin Kaepernick on 1 less carry in this game, running for 49 yards on 3 carries. Kaepernick went 39 yards on 4 carries, including 1 touchdown run and 1 lost fumble.

In the air, the 49ers had 2 players receiving for over 100 yards each. Michael Crabtree was the front-runner with 113 yards and 1 touchdown on 6 catches, followed closely by Vernon Davis with 106 yards on 5 receptions. Also making a significant contribution was Kyle Williams with 50 yards on 2 catches.

With 621 yards of total offense from 310 yards on the ground and 311 in the air, it's easy to see the San Francisco offense was well-balanced in this game. The 49ers also won the turnover war 2-1. As expected from the above numbers, San Francisco had much more time of possession, 36:17 to 23:43.

All told, the 49ers defense held the Bills to only 204 yards of total offense, meaning that at 621 of their own yards, they had 3 times the offensive yards of their opponent.

The kicking game was also perfect with David Akers hitting 1 of 1 field goals and 6 of 6 extra points.

While fans love shutouts, this victory was more impressive on all fronts than the previous week's shutout. The 49ers won by more points, put up a lot more yards, and dominated on all fronts.

Team Leaders

Passing

Alex Smith #11
303 Yards, 3 Touchdowns, 0 Interceptions
(18/24, Comp 75.00 %)

Colin Kaepernick #7
7 Yards, 0 Touchdowns, 0 Interceptions
(1/1, Comp 100.00 %)

2012 – 2013 San Francisco 49ers 31

Rushing

Frank Gore #21
64 Yards on 20 Carries
3.20 Yards per Carry
1 Rushing Touchdown

Kendall Hunter #32
56 Yards on 8 Carries
7.00 Yards per Carry
1 Rushing Touchdown

Colin Kaepernick #7
50 Yards on 5 Carries
10.00 Yards per Carry
1 Rushing Touchdown

Mario Manningham #82
28 Yards on 1 Carry
28.00 Yards per Carry
1 Rushing Touchdown

Receiving

Mario Manningham #82
47 Yards on 3 Receptions
15.67 Yards per Reception
0 Touchdown Receptions

Delanie Walker #46
31 Yards on 2 Receptions
15.50 Yards per Reception
0 Touchdown Receptions

Dan Fathow 32

Vernon Davis #85
28 Yards on 2 Receptions
14.00 Yards per Reception
0 Touchdown Receptions

Michael Crabtree #15
15 Yards on 2 Receptions
7.50 Yards per Reception
0 Touchdown Receptions

Kicking

David Akers #2
10 Points Total
2/4 Field Goals
5/4 Extra Points

Interceptions

Patrick Willis #52
1 Interception

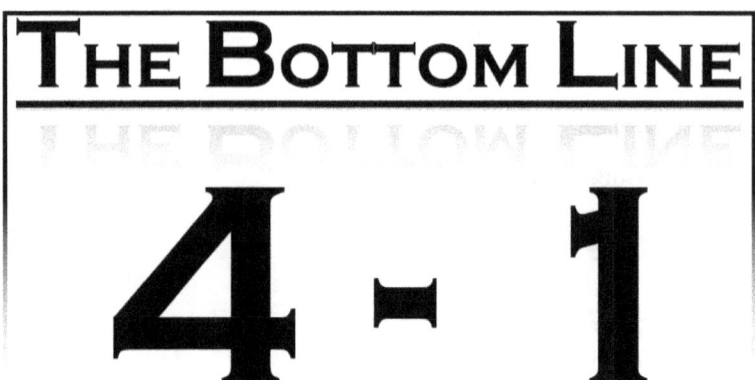

THE BOTTOM LINE

4 - 1

2012 – 2013 SAN FRANCISCO 49ERS 33

WEEK 6

October 14, 2012
Candlestick Park – San Francisco, CA

Teams	1st	2nd	3rd	4th	Total
New York Giants	0	10	13	3	26
San Frnacisco 49ers	3	0	0	0	3

GAME SUMMARY

After 2 weeks in a row of blowout victories, the 49ers lost to the Giants, being held to only a field goal. Coming into Week 6, the Giants were struggling a bit at 3-2, and the 49ers were at 4-1. A 23-point New York victory was a bit unexpected.

How on earth did that happen?

For starters, Alex Smith had a rough day, being intercepted on 3 occasions and being sacked 4 times. He was held to 200 yards and connected on 19 on 30 passes for a 63.33 completion percentage.

Colin Kaepernick was in the game, connecting on 4 of 7 passes for 82 yards. He was also sacked 2 times. Between Smith's and Kaepernick's sacks, the Giants defense got to 49ers quarterbacks 6 times in this game.

David Akers struggled in this game, going 1 for 3 on field goal attempts.

Total yards were close for both teams with the Giants having a slight edge of 342 to 314 yards. The 49ers losing the turnover battle 0-3 is what made the Giants' yardage count for 26 points, and San Francisco's similar yardage only count for 3.

TEAM LEADERS

Passing

Alex Smith #11
200 Yards, 0 Touchdowns, 3 Interceptions
(19/30, 63.33 Comp %)

Colin Kaepernick #7
82 Yards, 0 Touchdowns, 0 Interceptions
(4/7, Comp 57.14 %)

Rushing

Frank Gore #21
36 Yards on 8 Carries
4.50 Yards per Carry
0 Rushing Touchdowns

Kendall Hunter #32
26 Yards on 4 Carries
6.50 Yards per Carry
0 Rushing Touchdowns

Mario Manningham #82
7 Yards on 1 Carry
7.00 Yards per Carry
0 Rushing Touchdowns

2012 – 2013 San Francisco 49ers 35

Colin Kaepernick #7
6 Yards on 2 Carries
3.00 Yards per Carry
0 Rushing Touchdowns

Alex Smith #11
5 Yards on 2 Carries
2.50 Yards per Carry
0 Rushing Touchdowns

Receiving

Randy Moss #84
75 Yards on 2 Receptions
37.50 Yards per Reception
0 Touchdown Receptions

Mario Manningham #82
72 Yards on 5 Receptions
14.40 Yards per Reception
0 Touchdown Receptions

Kyle Williams #10
40 Yards on 4 Receptions
10.00 Yards per Reception
0 Touchdown Receptions

Vernon Davis #85
37 Yards on 3 Receptions
12.33 Yards per Reception
0 Touchdown Receptions

Michael Crabtree #15
26 Yards on 3 Receptions
8.67 Yards per Reception
0 Touchdown Receptions

Dan Fathow 36

Kicking

David Akers #2
3 Points Total
1/3 Field Goals
0/0 Extra Points

Interceptions

none

The Bottom Line

4 - 2

WEEK 7

October 18, 2012
Candlestick Park – San Francisco, CA

Teams	1st	2nd	3rd	4th	Total
Seattle Seahawks	3	3	0	0	6
San Francisco 49ers	3	0	7	3	13

GAME SUMMARY

Week 7 had the 4-2 Seahawks meeting the 4-2 49ers in Candlestick Park. The 49ers were coming off a frustrating loss to the Giants, and the Seahawks were coming off a gigantic win over the New England Patriots.

Most of this victory can be attributed to Frank Gore. Gore caught 16 passes for 131 yards, and he put up 51 additional rushing yards. His combined efforts added up to 181 total offensive yards. That's an impressive game.

Alex Smith had a modest day with 140 yards on 14 of 23 attempts for 1 touchdown and 1 interception. He did outperform his competition; Russell Wilson, who was only 9 of 23 for 122 yards, 0 touchdowns, and 1 interception.

San Francisco led in total yards (313-251), passing yards (138-115), and rushing yards (175-136). Turnovers were equal with 1 interception a piece. Time of possession was nearly equal with the 49ers having the ball for 3 minutes more than the

Seahawks. One telling factor was that San Francisco had 18 1st downs, while the Seahawks had only 13.

Kicker David Akers had a flawless day accounting for more than half of the 49ers' points from 2 of 2 field goals 1 of 1 extra points.

Team Leaders

Passing

Alex Smith #11
140 Yards, 1 Touchdown, 1 Interception
(14/23, 60.87 Comp %)

Rushing

Frank Gore #21
131 Yards on 16 Carries
8.19 Yards per Carry
0 Rushing Touchdowns

Kendall Hunter #32
31 Yards on 9 Carries
3.44 Yards per Carry
0 Rushing Touchdowns

Alex Smith #11
11 Yards on 5 Carries
2.20 Yards per Carry
0 Rushing Touchdowns

2012 – 2013 San Francisco 49ers 39

Kyle Williams #10
3 Yards on 1 Carry
3.00 Yards per Carry
0 Rushing Touchdowns

Colin Kaepernick #7
-1 Yards on 1 Carries
-1.00 Yards per Carry
0 Rushing Touchdowns

Receiving

Frank Gore #21
51 Yards on 5 Receptions
10.20 Yards per Reception
0 Touchdown Receptions

Michael Crabtree #15
31 Yards on 4 Receptions
7.75 Yards per Reception
0 Touchdown Receptions

Kyle Williams #10
18 Yards on 1 Reception
18.00 Yards per Reception
0 Touchdown Receptions

Delanie Walker #46
12 Yards on 1 Reception
12.00 Yards per Reception
1 Touchdown Reception

Dan Fathow 40

Kicking

David Akers #2
7 Points Total
2/2 Field Goals
1/1 Extra Points

Interceptions

Dashon Goldson #38
1 Interception

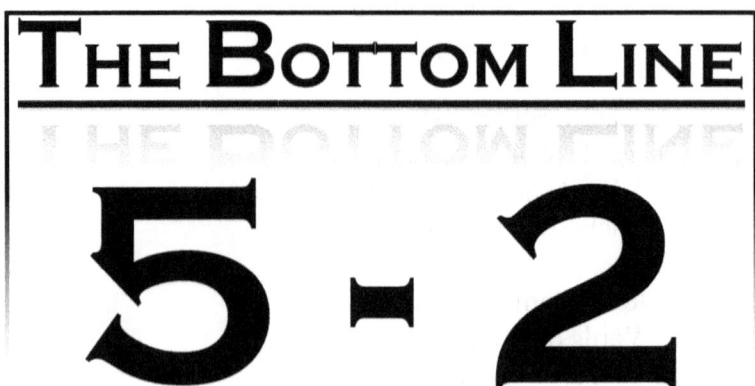

The Bottom Line

5 - 2

2012 – 2013 SAN FRANCISCO 49ERS 41

WEEK 8

October 29, 2012
University of Phoenix Stadium – Glendale, AZ

Teams	1st	2nd	3rd	4th	Total
Arizona Cardinals	0	0	3	0	3
San Francisco 49ers	7	10	7	0	24

GAME SUMMARY

Week 8 saw the 49ers return to top form and once again blow out its opponent. Coming into the game, the Arizona Cardinals were 4-3, and the 49ers were 5-2. At only 1 game apart between the 2 teams' records, this contest promised to be more competitive than it was.

Alex Smith may have thrown for less yards than his competitor, but he had a much better game. Smith connected on an amazing 18 of 19 passes for 232 yards, 3 touchdowns, and 0 interceptions. Arizona quarterback John Skelton threw for 290 yards, but they came on 32 of 53 passes, and 1 interception with 0 touchdowns. 3 touchdowns with 0 interceptions will nearly always produce better results than 0 touchdowns and 1 interception, regardless of the yardage involved. Smith's 94.74 completion percentage was a truly amazing accomplishment, coming darn close to perfection.

Michael Crabtree had a great game, catching 5 passes for 72 yards and 2 touchdowns. Randy Moss also got into the end zone on a long, 47-yard reception.

Even though all 3 touchdowns came in the air, the ground game was working too. Frank Gore rushed for 55 yards, and Kendall Hunter rushed for 43 yards.

Team Leaders

Passing

Alex Smith #11
232 Yards, 3 Touchdowns, 0 Interceptions
(18/19, 94.74 Comp %)

Rushing

Frank Gore #21
55 Yards on 16 Carries
3.44 Yards per Carry
0 Rushing Touchdowns

Kendall Hunter #32
43 Yards on 10 Carries
4.30 Yards per Carry
0 Rushing Touchdowns

Michael Crabtree #15
8 Yards on 1 Carry
8.00 Yards per Carry
0 Rushing Touchdowns

2012 – 2013 San Francisco 49ers 43

Alex Smith #11
6 Yards on 1 Carry
6.00 Yards per Carry
0 Rushing Touchdowns

Receiving

Michael Crabtree #15
72 Yards on 5 Receptions
14.40 Yards per Reception
2 Touchdown Receptions

Randy Moss #84
47 Yards on 1 Reception
47.00 Yards per Reception
1 Touchdown Reception

Delanie Walker #46
38 Yards on 2 Receptions
19.00 Yards per Reception
0 Touchdown Receptions

Vernon Davis #85
34 Yards on 2 Receptions
17.00 Yards per Reception
0 Touchdown Receptions

Kicking

David Akers #2
6 Points Total
1/1 Field Goals
3/3 Extra Points

DAN FATHOW 44

Interceptions

Chris Culliver #29
1 Interception

THE BOTTOM LINE

6 - 2

WEEK 10

November 11, 2012
Candlestick Park – San Francisco, CA

Teams	1st	2nd	3rd	4th	OT	Total
St. Louis Rams	14	0	3	7	0	24
San Francisco 49ers	0	7	0	17	0	24

GAME SUMMARY

This game was the 1st tie in the NFL in 4 years. The St. Louis Rams were only 3-5 coming into this game, but one can never underestimate the importance of a divisional rivalry and the ability of players to raise the level of their performance in such a game. After all, the struggling New Orleans Saints at 4-4, dealt their rival, undefeated Atlanta Falcons their first loss of 2012.

Although this game was a tie, the Rams had the leading passer, rusher, and receiver in this contest. Steven Jackson rushed for 101 yards and 1 touchdown on 29 carries. Danny Amendola caught 11 passes for 102 yards. And, quarterback Sam Bradford threw for 275 yards and 2 touchdowns with 0 interceptions, while being sacked twice.

St. Louis won on total yards and passing yards, but the 49ers won the rushing game (183-159), the penalty battle (66 yards to 85 yards), and the turnover war (0-1).

Both teams' kickers missed attempts to win the game with a field goal in overtime.

The most heartbreaking part of the game was absolutely Alex Smith suffering a concussion, which not only made him come out of the game, not only changed the life of Colin Kaepernick, not only changed the course of his career, but has become an increasingly terrifying injury with the recent links between concussions and long-term mental and physical illness.

It was an unexpectedly hard game and a sad day for 49ers fans.

Team Leaders

Passing

Alex Smith #11
72 Yards, 1 Touchdown, 0 Interceptions
(7/8, 87.50 Comp %)

Colin Kaepernick #7
117 Yards, 0 Touchdowns, 0 Interceptions
(11/17, 64.71 Comp %)

Rushing

Frank Gore #21
97 Yards on 21 Carries
4.62 Yards per Carry
1 Rushing Touchdown

2012 – 2013 San Francisco 49ers 47

Colin Kaepernick #7
66 Yards on 8 Carries
8.25 Yards per Carry
1 Rushing Touchdown

Kendall Hunter #32
15 Yards on 3 Carries
5.00 Yards per Carry
0 Rushing Touchdowns

Alex Smith #11
5 Yards on 2 Carries
2.50 Yards per Carry
0 Rushing Touchdowns

Receiving

Michael Crabtree #15
70 Yards on 5 Receptions
14.00 Yards per Reception
1 Touchdown Reception

Vernon Davis #85
30 Yards on 4 Receptions
7.50 Yards per Reception
0 Touchdown Receptions

Kyle Williams #10
24 Yards on 2 Receptions
12.00 Yards per Reception
0 Touchdown Receptions

Mario Manningham #82
20 Yards on 1 Reception
20.00 Yards per Reception
0 Touchdown Receptions

Dan Fathow 48

Randy Moss #84
19 Yards on 2 Reception
9.50 Yards per Reception
0 Touchdown Receptions

Kicking

David Akers #2
6 Points Total
1/2 Field Goals
3/3 Extra Points

Interceptions

none

Week 11

November 19, 2012
Candlestick Park – San Francisco, CA

Teams	1st	2nd	3rd	4th	Total
Chicago Bears	0	0	7	0	7
San Francisco 49ers	10	10	7	5	32

GAME SUMMARY

With starting quarterback Alex Smith out with a concussion, there were a lot of unknown variables coming into this game. Fortunately for 49ers fans, the unknown was all in San Francisco's favor.

Colin Kaepernick stepped up to lead the team to a crushing victory over the Chicago Bears. In his first game as a full-time starter, Kaepernick put up 243 yards on 16 of 23 passes. His 69.57% completion percentage rivaled Smith's league leading 70.18%.

The 49ers defense showed up in force, holding Jason Campbell and the Bears to only 7 points, including 3 shutout quarters and a completely shutout first half. On the ground, Chicago only mustered 85 rushing yards, including 13 from backup quarterback Jason Campbell. In the air, Campbell only put up 107 yards with 1 touchdown and 2 interceptions.

The 49ers won total yards 353 to 143 yards, which was 2.5 times more offense than the Bears could put up. The 49ers led both on passing and rushing yards. They also won the turnover battle 0-2.

For those who were worried that the 49ers would fall apart without Alex Smith; Colin Kaepernick, the 49ers offense, and the 49ers defense all put in an impressive performance to prove that San Francisco was still a dangerous team and a serious post-season threat.

Team Leaders

Passing

Colin Kaepernick #7
243 Yards, 2 Touchdowns, 0 Interceptions
(16/23, 69.57 Comp %)

Rushing

Frank Gore #21
78 Yards on 17 Carries
4.59 Yards per Carry
0 Rushing Touchdowns

Kendall Hunter #32
27 Yards on 5 Carries
5.40 Yards per Carry
1 Rushing Touchdown

Colin Kaepernick #7
10 Yards on 4 Carries
2.50 Yards per Carry
0 Rushing Touchdowns

2012 – 2013 San Francisco 49ers 51

Receiving

Vernon Davis #85
83 Yards on 6 Receptions
13.83 Yards per Reception
1 Touchdown Reception

Kyle Williams #10
60 Yards on 2 Receptions
30.00 Yards per Reception
0 Touchdown Receptions

Mario Manningham #82
45 Yards on 2 Receptions
22.50 Yards per Reception
0 Touchdown Receptions

Michael Crabtree #15
31 Yards on 3 Receptions
10.33 Yards per Reception
1 Touchdown Reception

Randy Moss #84
12 Yards on 1 Reception
12.00 Yards per Reception
0 Touchdown Receptions

Kicking

David Akers #2
12 Points Total
3/3 Field Goals
3/3 Extra Points

DAN FATHOW 52

Interceptions

Tarell Brown #25
1 Interception

Dashon Goldson #38
1 Interception

THE BOTTOM LINE
7 - 2 - 1

2012 – 2013 San Francisco 49ers 53

Week 12

November 25, 2012
Mercedes-Benz Superdome – New Orleans, LA

Teams	1st	2nd	3rd	4th	Total
New Orleans Saints	7	7	7	0	21
San Francisco 49ers	7	7	14	3	31

GAME SUMMARY

Week 12 saw the 49ers traveling to New Orleans to meet the Saints, who had just evened their record up at 5-5, which is deceptive considering the Saints were on a 3-game winning streak, including having beaten the undefeated Atlanta Falcons.

The 7-2-1 49ers were certainly the favorites in this contest, even with Alex Smith not playing. The Saints were obviously struggling with the aftereffects of the infamous bounty scandal, which resulted in head coach Sean Payton being suspended for the entire season, contributing to the Saints unexpectedly starting the season 0-4, which was a huge hole to try and climb out of.

What was deceptive and dangerous about this inconsistent Saints team was that they were 1st in the NFL in passing yards with a 312 passing-yards-per-game average. Unfortunately for them by season's end, their defense allowed the most yards in NFL history at 7,042 yards, with a 440.13 yards-allowed-per-game average. So, basically, the 49ers were meeting the best passing offense in the league and the worst defense in NFL history at the same time. In retrospect, it's amazing the Drew-Brees-led offense were able to carry that defense to a 7-9 record. The previous record holders were the 1981 Baltimore Colts, who finished with a 2-14 record for their efforts.

On a good day, the Saints could beat anyone. On a bad day, they could truly lose to anyone, even the worst team in the league. That makes for a hard opponent to prepare for, as you have no idea which version you're going to face that day.

This game proved to be a back-and-forth shootout. In the first quarter, both teams scored a touchdown. The second quarter went exactly the same way, ending the first half at 14-14. In the third quarter, the 49ers pulled away, and the Saints never caught up again.

Colin Kaepernick had a good day in the air, connecting on 16 of 25 passes for 231 yards, 1 touchdown, and 1 interception. On the ground, Kaepernick ran 6 times for 27 yards and a touchdown. All in all, it was a solid performance from a new starter.

In 2012, opposing quarterback Drew Brees led the league for the second year in a row in passing yards with 5,177 and in touchdowns with 43. That works out to be 323.56 yards and 2.69 passing touchdowns per game. The 49ers defense held him to only 267 yards, which is 56.6 yards below his average. While Brees did connect for 3 touchdowns, which was slightly above his average, the San Francisco defense forced 2 interceptions, which is nearly double Brees's average. So, the San Francisco defense did a good job containing a top-performing quarterback in this victory.

On the ground, the 49ers shut New Orleans's running game down, only allowing 59 yards. On the other side of the ball, San Francisco rushed for 144 yards, more than double what the Saints were able to do. 83 of those yards belonged to Frank Gore.

In the air, the 49ers put up 231 yards. 81 of them went to Delanie Walker, and 69 went to Mario Manningham.

The 49ers were much better on 3rd-down conversions, being successful on 6 of 13 attempts, while the Saints only mustered 3 of 11. San Francisco won on total yards (375-290), tied on passing yards, and won big on rushing yards. Even though the 49ers had 6 more penalties than New Orleans, the results were only 15 more penalty yards. The turnover battle was even at 2-2, and time of possession was nearly identical with the 49ers having the ball for 12 more seconds than New Orleans.

What was even more impressive about the 49ers defense in this contest was that both interceptions were run back for touchdowns, accounting for 14 of San Francisco's 31 points. Keep in mind that this was a 10-point victory, and those 2 defensive touchdowns become all the more important.

One of the only points of concern for the 49ers in this game was David Akers's kicking. He went 1 for 3 on the day, which isn't too much of a reason for alarm, but when one remembers he missed the opportunity to win the tie game to St. Louis in overtime, his reliability becomes somewhat questionable.

Even though the Saints were undeniably struggling through a difficult year, this was a solid victory for the 49ers. San Francisco played well on both sides of the ball. Winning by 10 points in the Superdome and keeping New Orleans to under 300 total yards on offense are accomplishments that should not be taken lightly. The 49ers handled a top-rated offense on the road while being led by a new quarterback; that is a sign of a championship team.

Team Leaders

Passing

Colin Kaepernick #7
231 Yards, 1 Touchdown, 1 Interception
(16/25, 64.00 Comp %)

Rushing

Frank Gore #21
83 Yards on 19 Carries
4.37 Yards per Carry
0 Rushing Touchdowns

Kendall Hunter #32
28 Yards on 4 Carries
7.00 Yards per Carry
0 Rushing Touchdowns

Colin Kaepernick #7
27 Yards on 6 Carries
4.50 Yards per Carry
1 Rushing Touchdown

Receiving

Delanie Walker #46
81 Yards on 3 Receptions
27.00 Yards per Reception
0 Touchdown Receptions

2012 – 2013 SAN FRANCISCO 49ERS 57

Mario Manningham #82
69 Yards on 5 Receptions
13.80 Yards per Reception
0 Touchdown Receptions

Bruce Miller #49
37 Yards on 3 Receptions
12.33 Yards per Reception
0 Touchdown Receptions

Michael Crabtree #15
26 Yards on 3 Receptions
8.67 Yards per Reception
0 Touchdown Receptions

Frank Gore #21
18 Yards on 2 Receptions
9.00 Yards per Reception
1 Touchdown Reception

Kicking

David Akers #2
7 Points Total
1/3 Field Goals
4/4 Extra Points

Interceptions

Ahmad Brooks #55
1 Interception Run back for a Touchdown

Donte Whitner # 31
1 Interception Run back for a Touchdown

Dan Fathow 58

The Bottom Line

8 - 2 - 1

WEEK 13

December 2, 2012
Edward Jones Dome – St. Louis, MO

Teams	1st	2nd	3rd	4th	OT	Total
St. Louis Rams	0	0	2	11	3	16
San Francisco 49ers	7	0	0	6	0	20

GAME SUMMARY

At this point in the season, the 49ers were 8-2-1, but they were 4-0-1 in their last 5 games. If not for the tie to their opponent 3 weeks prior, San Francisco would be 5-0 in their last 5 games.

The Rams were 4-6-1 coming into this game. They would eventually end up 7-8-1, nearly finishing up at .500, so it wasn't the best year for St. Louis. The highlights of their season thus far included beating the Washington Redskins in Week 2, the Seattle Seahawks in Week 4, and the tie to the 49ers in Week 10. Despite their record, 2 of the Rams' 4 victories were against playoff teams, and their 1 overtime tie was against a Super Bowl-bound team. They could certainly perform better than their record indicated, as would be the case this day.

San Francisco jumped out in front, scoring an unanswered touchdown in the first quarter. The second quarter would be scoreless, going into the second half with the 49ers up

7-0. Things would begin to go wrong when the inexperienced Kaepernick was called for intentional grounding in the end zone, which resulted in a 2-point safety.

With the score at 7-2 at the start of the 4th quarter, things were still looking good for the 49ers. On the 49ers first possession, things looked even better as David Akers hit a 23-yard field goal to bring the score up to 10-2.

Close to their own end zone, the 49ers lost the ball as Kaepernick fumbled. Janoris Jenkins picked up the ball and ran it in for a touchdown, which would be the only Rams touchdown of the day. The Rams successfully went for a 2-point conversion, which tied the score at 10-10.

David Akers kicked a field goal to give the 49ers the lead at 13-10.

The Rams drove down the field from their own 20 yard-line to the San Francisco 35. With only 2 seconds left on the clock, rookie kicker Greg Zuerlein hit a 53-yard field goal to send the game into overtime.

Once again, David Akers found himself in overtime with a chance to kick a field goal to give the 49ers a win over the Rams. Unfortunately, once again, he missed the kick, this time from 51 yards away.

St. Louis Rams' kicker Greg Zuerlein sealed the game with a 54-yard field goal with 26 seconds left in overtime.

Colin Kaepernick was not terribly effective in the air in this game, throwing for 208 yards and 0 touchdowns. He was sacked 3 times in this contest. His biggest contribution came in the form of his rushing attack, which made him the game's leading rusher at 84 yards. Kaepernick's 4th-quarter fumble was crucial in this loss, giving the Rams their only touchdown of the day.

The last time these 2 teams met, kicker David Akers had a shaky game, failing to win the game in overtime with a field goal. In this contest, he went 2 for 3 on field goals and 1 of 1 on extra points, accounting for 7 of the Rams' 13 points. Unfortunately for him and 49ers fans, his missed field goal was in overtime and cost the team the win.

In this contest, the 49ers won total yards (339-293), rushing yards (148-85), and 3rd down efficiency (8-19 to 3-16). While many may blame the entire loss on Akers' missed field goal, Kaepernick's fumble for a Rams' touchdown and safety for 2 points were key mistakes in this loss.

There were great things for the 49ers in this game, despite the bitter ending. Michael Crabtree caught for 101 yards, averaging 14.43 yards per catch. And despite his critical mistakes, Kaepernick rushed for 84 yards, giving glimpses of his record-setting rushing to come in the playoffs. When your quarterback is getting a 9.33 average-yards-per-carry, it makes for exciting play, regardless of the outcome of the game.

Team Leaders

Passing

Colin Kaepernick #7
208 Yards, 0 Touchdowns, 0 Interceptions
(21/32, 65.63 Comp %)

Rushing

Colin Kaepernick #7
84 Yards on 9 Carries
9.33 Yards per Carry
1 Rushing Touchdown

Frank Gore #21
23 Yards on 58 Carries
2.52 Yards per Carry
1 Rushing Touchdown

Dan Fathow 62

Receiving

Michael Crabtree #15
101 Yards on 7 Receptions
14.43 Yards per Reception
0 Touchdown Receptions

Mario Manningham #82
37 Yards on 5 Receptions
7.40 Yards per Reception
0 Touchdown Receptions

Randy Moss #84
30 Yards on 3 Receptions
10.00 Yards per Reception
0 Touchdown Receptions

Bruce Miller #49
17 Yards on 2 Receptions
8.50 Yards per Reception
0 Touchdown Receptions

Kicking

David Akers #2
7 Points Total
2/3 Field Goals
1/1 Extra Points

2012 – 2013 SAN FRANCISCO 49ERS 63

Interceptions

none

THE BOTTOM LINE

8 - 3 - 1

Week 14

December 9, 2012
Candlestick Park – San Francisco, CA

Teams	1st	2nd	3rd	4th	Total
Miami Dolphins	0	3	3	7	**13**
San Francisco 49ers	0	6	7	14	**27**

GAME SUMMARY

This was not a high-flying game as both quarterbacks were limited to very light passing yards, Tannehill at 150 yards and Kaepernick at 185 yards.

Colin Kaepernick may have had remarkably low passing yards in this game and no passing touchdowns, but he did rush for 53 yards on 6 carries for 1 touchdown. However, he again fumbled the ball. In Kaepernick's defense, he did have a 78.26 completion percentage in this outing.

Along with Kaepernick, Frank Gore and Anthony Dixon had rushing touchdowns. Gore was the highest rusher for the 49ers with 63 yards, and he also caught 2 passes for an additional 22 yards of offense.

Michael Crabtree had a great day, making 9 grabs for 93 yards, and he was followed by Randy Moss who made 2 catches for 30 yards.

The kicking game was solid with David Akers having a perfect performance of hitting 2 of 2 field goals and 3 of 3 extra points.

In his last 3 games as a starter, Colin Kaepernick had passed for an average of 208 yards per game, and more relevant to the current situation, he had only an average of 196.5 passing yards per game in the past 2 games. On top of that, Kaepernick had only 1 passing touchdown and 1 interception in the past 3 games. That's not very impressive.

The above stats made it hard for some fans to accept Coach Harbaugh's decision to snub Alex Smith for this newcomer, who was putting up much lower passing statistics.

A 14-point victory was exactly what the 49ers needed after the painful overtime loss to St. Louis the week before. The only thing more the 49ers could have asked for in this contest would have been a passing touchdown, but, regardless, it was a solid victory.

Team Leaders

Passing

Colin Kaepernick #7
185 Yards, 0 Touchdowns, 0 Interceptions
(18/23, 78.26 Comp %)

Rushing

Frank Gore #21
63 Yards on 12 Carries
5.25 Yards per Carry
1 Rushing Touchdown

DAN FATHOW 66

Colin Kaepernick #7
53 Yards on 6 Carries
8.83 Yards per Carry
1 Rushing Touchdown

LaMichael James #23
30 Yards on 8 Carries
3.75 Yards per Carry
0 Rushing Touchdowns

Anthony Dixon #24
9 Yards on 2 Carries
4.50 Yards per Carry
1 Rushing Touchdown

Receiving

Michael Crabtree #15
93 Yards on 9 Receptions
10.33 Yards per Reception
0 Touchdown Receptions

Randy Moss #84
30 Yards on 2 Receptions
15.00 Yards per Reception
0 Touchdown Receptions

Frank Gore #21
22 Yards on 2 Receptions
11.00 Yards per Reception
0 Touchdown Receptions

2012 – 2013 San Francisco 49ers 67

Kicking

David Akers #2
9 Points Total
2/2 Field Goals
3/3 Extra Points

Interceptions

none

The Bottom Line

9 - 3 - 1

Week 15

December 16, 2012
Gillette Stadium – Foxboro, MA

Teams	1st	2nd	3rd	4th	Total
New England Patriots	0	3	7	24	**34**
San Francisco 49ers	7	10	14	10	**41**

GAME SUMMARY

This game was a great demonstration of the power the 2012 San Francisco 49ers had. Many critics thought that the New England Patriots were a superior team and would provide the litmus test to prove that the 49ers were not a Super Bowl contender. Boy, were they wrong.

On the road in Foxboro, the 49ers jumped ahead of the Patriots 7-0. The 49ers defense was really on top of their game, ending the first half with only allowing the Tom Brady-led offense to score 1 field goal. That is no small accomplishment. The San Francisco offense was also firing, scoring 10 more points in the second quarter, giving them a 17-3 lead at halftime.

The second-half was truly a gunfight with New England rallying back with 31 points, and the 49ers responding with 24 points of their own to keep a 7-point lead and secure an important victory.

This game was exactly what the 49ers could have hoped for in beating the Patriots on the road. Colin Kaepernick answered some critics with 4 touchdown passes. True, he did only muster 221 passing yards with 1 interception, but he responded with poise when a Tom Brady-led offense came gunning back at them in the second half. A lesser quarterback with Kaepernick's limited experience would have crumbled under that kind of pressure. Instead, Kaepernick stuck to the gameplan and performed well.

A key factor in this impressive victory was that the 49ers won the turnover war 2-4, 2 of which were interceptions picked off Tom Brady. Time of possession was nearly identical, but New England soundly won total yards (520-388) and passing yards (425-208). This was where the 4 turnovers were crucial in making the Patriots throw yards away without putting anything to show for them on the scoreboard. However, the 49ers rushed for nearly double, racking up 180 yards, while holding that Pats to just 95 yards. What really allowed the Patriots to even make this a close game, despite the turnover debacle was that they were 4-5 in the red zone, while the 49ers were 1-4 in front of the end zone. The 49ers were much better on 3rd-down conversions with more than twice as many as the Patriots, going 5 for 14, while New England only mustered 2 of 15.

This game was undeniable proof that the 49ers were a championship team, deserving of respect from both sports fans and all opponents.

TEAM LEADERS

Passing

Colin Kaepernick #7
221 Yards, 4 Touchdowns, 1 Interception
(14/25, 56.00 Comp %)

Rushing

Frank Gore #21
83 Yards on 21 Carries
3.92 Yards per Carry
0 Rushing Touchdowns

LaMichael James #23
31 Yards on 8 Carries
3.88 Yards per Carry
0 Rushing Touchdowns

Dashon Goldson #38
31 Yards on 1 Carry
31.00 Yards per Carry
0 Rushing Touchdowns

Colin Kaepernick #7
28 Yards on 7 Carries
4.00 Yards per Carry
0 Rushing Touchdowns

Receiving

Michael Crabtree #15
107 Yards on 7 Receptions
15.29 Yards per Reception
2 Touchdown Receptions

Randy Moss #84
36 Yards on 2 Receptions
13.00 Yards per Reception
1 Touchdown Reception

2012 – 2013 San Francisco 49ers 71

Delanie Walker #46
34 Yards on 2 Receptions
17.00 Yards per Reception
1 Touchdown Reception

Frank Gore #21
34 Yards on 2 Receptions
17.00 Yards per Reception
0 Touchdown Receptions

Kicking

David Akers #2
11 Points Total
2/3 Field Goals
5/5 Extra Points

Interceptions

Carlos Rogers #22
1 Interception

Aldon Smith #99
1 Interception

The Bottom Line

10 - 3 - 1

Week 16

December 23, 2012
CenturyLink Field – Seattle, WA

Teams	1st	2nd	3rd	4th	Total
Seattle Seahawks	14	14	7	7	42
San Francisco 49ers	0	6	0	7	13

GAME SUMMARY

The 49ers caught the eye of the entire sports world with their victory over the Patriots in the previous week. Meeting the Seattle Seahawks was a high-profile game, being a significant test for both great teams.

Seattle was a hot team, coming into this game with a 9-5 record. While it was not as good as the 49ers 10-3-1, the Seahawks were particularly dangerous at home, with a 7-0 record while playing in Seattle.

While Kaepernick picked up his passing yardage slightly in this game to 244 yards, his completion percentage plummeted to 52.77. He threw for a passing touchdown, but his 1 interception nearly makes that a wash. These kinds of stats were what continued to fuel the heated debate over Alex Smith being snubbed from his starting position following his concussion.

Seattle did a great job on stopping the 49ers' typically strong running game. The 49ers were limited to a total of 82 rushing yards. The leading rusher was quarterback Colin Kaepernick with 31 yards, followed closely behind by Frank Gore with 28 yards.

San Francisco's kicking game did not instill a tremendous amount of confidence for fans, as kicker David Akers went 2 for 3 on field goals for the second week in a row.

The 49ers won the passing game 231 to 170 yards, but they lost on penalties, turnovers (0-1), total yards (313 to 346 yards), running yards (82 to 176 yards), and 3rd-down conversions (3/11 to 11/13). Seattle going 11 for 13 on 3rd-down conversions was a huge difference in this game, helping make their yardage count for more on the scoreboard.

Coming off the big victory over the Patriots, this was a disappointing loss that was a bit of an upset. While the statistics fueled the fire of the heated quarterback situation, the 49ers were still 10-4-1 and in good shape to destroy some opponents in the post season.

Team Leaders

Passing

Colin Kaepernick #7
244 Yards, 1 Touchdown, 1 Interception
(19/36, 52.77 Comp %)

Rushing

Colin Kaepernick #7
31 Yards on 7 Carries
4.43 Yards per Carry
0 Rushing Touchdowns

Frank Gore #21
28 Yards on 6 Carries
4.67 Yards per Carry
0 Rushing Touchdowns

LaMichael James #23
15 Yards on 4 Carries
3.75 Yards per Carry
0 Rushing Touchdowns

Receiving

Michael Crabtree #15
65 Yards on 4 Receptions
16.25 Yards per Reception
0 Touchdown Receptions

Delanie Walker #46
54 Yards on 4 Receptions
13.50 Yards per Reception
1 Touchdown Reception

Randy Moss #84
44 Yards on 3 Receptions
14.67 Yards per Reception
0 Touchdown Receptions

Garrett Celek #81
41 Yards on 2 Receptions
20.50 Yards per Reception
0 Touchdown Receptions

2012 – 2013 San Francisco 49ers 75

Kicking

David Akers #2
7 Points Total
2/3 Field Goals
1/1 Extra Points

Interceptions

Patrick Willis #52
1 Interception

The Bottom Line

10 - 4 - 1

DAN FATHOW 76

WEEK 17

December 30, 2012
Paul Brown Stadium – Cincinnati, OH

Teams	1st	2nd	3rd	4th	Total
Cincinnati Bengals	0	7	6	10	23
Baltimore Ravens	7	0	0	10	17

GAME SUMMARY

San Francisco didn't really have anything to prove to anyone in this game. With an 11-4-1 record versus the 5-11 Cardinals (who were 1-7 on the road, by the way), all they really had to do was not lose. However, after the loss to the Seahawks in the previous week, displaying some explosive firepower would be great for team momentum, confidence, and fan excitement.

The 49ers won total yards 407 to 262 yards, passing yards 278-207, and rushing yards 129 to 55 yards. In addition to the offensive domination, San Francisco won the turnover war 0-2. Another telling statistic attesting to the 49ers' dominance in this outing was that Arizona only had 11 1st downs while they had 20. When you have nearly twice the 1st downs as your opponent, you're going to win the large majority of the time.

Colin Kaepernick threw for 276 yards with a 57.14 completion percentage with 2 touchdowns and 0 interceptions.

While the completion percentage was poor, Kaepernick slung the ball into the end zone for 2 touchdowns, which was an improvement and a healthy sign of his abilities going into the post season.

Kaepernick only carried the ball 3 times in this contest, which was a wise decision to avoid unnecessary injury for the playoffs.

Michael Crabtree had a banner day catching 8 passes for 172 yards and 2 touchdowns, including one long 49-yard reception.

The San Francisco defense had a strong showing, holding the Cardinals to only 262 total yards of offense, 207 in the air and a mere 55 yards on the ground.

The turnover war was also won by the 49ers 0-2, forcing 1 fumble and 1 interception.

Once again, the only area of real concern for San Francisco was its kicking performance. David Akers went 2 for 4 on field goals in this game.

While having not attempted many 4th-down conversions this season, the 49ers went 2 for 2 on 4th-down in this contest, which was a great accomplishment to achieve going into the playoffs.

Team Leaders

Passing

Colin Kaepernick #7
276 Yards, 2 Touchdowns, 0 Interceptions
(16/28, 57.14 Comp %)

Alex Smith #11
6 Yards, 0 Touchdowns, 0 Interceptions
(1/1, 100.00 Comp %)

Dan Fathow 78

Rushing

Frank Gore #21
68 Yards on 20 Carries
3.40 Yards per Carry
1 Rushing Touchdown

LaMichael James #23
49 Yards on 7 Carries
7.00 Yards per Carry
0 Rushing Touchdowns

Receiving

Michael Crabtree #15
172 Yards on 8 Receptions
21.50 Yards per Reception
2 Touchdown Receptions

Delanie Walker #46
50 Yards on 2 Receptions
25.00 Yards per Reception
0 Touchdown Receptions

Randy Moss #84
28 Yards on 2 Receptions
14.00 Yards per Reception
0 Touchdown Receptions

Frank Gore #21
21 Yards on 3 Receptions
7.00 Yards per Reception
0 Touchdown Receptions

2012 – 2013 San Francisco 49ers 79

Kicking

David Akers #2
9 Points Total
2/4 Field Goals
3/3 Extra Points

Interceptions

Tarell Brown #25
1 Interception

The Bottom Line

11 - 4 - 1

Week 18

January 12, 2013
Candlestick Park – San Francisco, CA

Teams	1st	2nd	3rd	4th	Total
Green Bay Packers	14	7	3	7	**31**
San Francisco 49ers	7	17	7	14	**45**

GAME SUMMARY

On January 12, 2013, the San Francisco 49ers dove headfirst into the post season, meeting the Green Bay Packers at home. The Packers' regular season record was 11-5, which was slightly better than the 49ers 11-4-1. A factor that should have been taken into account by the media was that this was a home game for the 49ers, and the 49ers were 6-1-1 at home while the Packers were only 4-4 on the road. However, the Packers were heavy favorites in this game.

With the power of both teams' hefty defenses, very few people were expecting 76 total points in this contest. Coming into this game, the Packers were 17th against allowing rushing yards, with an average of 118.5 yards per game. However in this outing, the 49ers ran all over them to the tune of 323 yards, which was nearly 3 times their season average.

2012 – 2013 San Francisco 49ers 81

How did the 49ers put up such amazing numbers on the ground?

More than half of the team's rushing yards came under the feet of quarterback Colin Kaepernick, who racked up 181 yards and 2 touchdowns on 16 carries for an average of 11.31 yards per carry. When your quarterback is averaging a little more than a 1st down every time he runs the ball, you're onto something amazing.

What was equally unbelievable was that, even though Kaepernick almost rushed for 200 yards, Frank Gore also ran for over 119 yards of his own. Between the 2 of them, they accounted for an even 300 rushing yards out of the team's 323 total yards on the ground.

In the air, the 49ers were strong, catching 17 balls for 263 yards. The big star here was clearly Michael Crabtree who caught 9 passes for 119 yards for an average of 13.22 yards per reception. On top of his 119 rushing yards, Frank Gore also caught 2 passes for 48 yards, giving him a total of 167 total offensive yards. It also marked the second game in a row in which Crabtree caught 2 touchdown passes.

David Akers had a solid day, going 1 for 1 on field goals and 6 for 6 on extra points.

Despite losing by 14 points, opposing quarterback Aaron Rodgers threw for 257 yards on 26 of 39 pass attempts for 2 touchdowns and 1 interception. His completion percentage was 66.67.

Colin Kaepernick threw for more yardage with 263 yards. He had one less touchdown than Rodgers (1-2), and they were tied on interceptions at 1 apiece. Both quarterbacks were sacked once. Kaepernick had a lower 54.84 completion percentage, which was 12 percent lower than Rodgers, but the obvious difference was that Rodgers didn't rush for 181 yards and 2 touchdowns as Kaepernick did, which was a quarterback record.

In conclusion, it was an awesome showing for the 49ers, solidly beating a great team, and it was specifically a fantastic showing for Colin Kaepernick, who demonstrated a strong argument as to why he was given the starting position over Alex Smith.

Dan Fathow 82

Team Leaders

Passing

Colin Kaepernick #7
263 Yards, 2 Touchdowns, 1 Interception
(17/31, 54.84 Comp %)

Rushing

Colin Kaepernick #7
181 Yards on 16 Carries
11.31 Yards per Carry
2 Rushing Touchdowns

Frank Gore #21
119 Yards on 23 Carries
5.17 Yards per Carry
1 Rushing Touchdown

LaMichael James #23
21 Yards on 3 Carries
7.00 Yards per Carry
0 Rushing Touchdowns

Receiving

Michael Crabtree #15
119 Yards on 9 Receptions
13.22 Yards per Reception
2 Touchdown Receptions

2012 – 2013 San Francisco 49ers 83

Frank Gore #21
48 Yards on 2 Receptions
24.00 Yards per Reception
0 Touchdown Receptions

Vernon Davis #85
44 Yards on 1 Reception
44.00 Yards per Reception
0 Touchdown Receptions

Randy Moss #84
25 Yards on 2 Receptions
12.50 Yards per Reception
0 Touchdown Receptions

Kicking

David Akers #2
9 Points Total
2/4 Field Goals
3/3 Extra Points

Interceptions

Tarell Brown #25
1 Interception

DAN FATHOW 84

THE BOTTOM LINE

12 - 4 - 1

WEEK 19

January 20, 2013
Georgia Dome – Atlanta, GA

Teams	1st	2nd	3rd	4th	Total
Atlanta Falcons	10	14	0	0	**24**
San Francisco 49ers	0	14	7	7	**28**

GAME SUMMARY

The NFC Championship Game saw the San Francisco 49ers meeting the Atlanta Falcons on the road in the Georgia Dome.

The Atlanta Falcons were undefeated for a large chunk of the season, going 8-0 before losing to their rival New Orleans Saints on the road. Despite finishing with the best record in all of football at 13-3, the Atlanta Falcons had been fighting all season for respect from the sports media, arguably being the least-respected 13-win team in NFL history.

On offense, the Falcons were 6th in overall passing yards, averaging 282 yards per game. However, on the ground, they were 29th in rushing with 87 yards per game. On defense, they were 23rd against the pass, and against the ground attack, they were 21st overall, allowing 123 yards per game. So, clearly, the team wasn't particularly balanced, relying mostly on its passing strengths to win games.

Besides harsh criticisms of their impressive record in 2012, the Falcons were known as being a team that could not win in the playoffs, particularly branded as starting strong but not being able to hold onto a lead against a good team. That label would prove true in this contest, further strengthening this psychological "curse" against them in the future.

The game started off as many had predicted with Atlanta jumping out ahead with a field goal and a touchdown, leading the 49ers 10-0 in the first quarter. In the second quarter, the 49ers offense took off, putting 2 touchdowns on the board. Unfortunately, the Falcons also scored 2 touchdowns, holding onto their 10-point lead, closing out the half with a score of 24-14.

The second half also went exactly as many had predicted. Atlanta had a lead and slowly let it deteriorate. The 49ers scored a touchdown in the 3rd quarter and another in the 4th, all the while shutting the Falcons out, keeping them scoreless for the rest of the game. The final score was 28-24 in favor of San Francisco.

Colin Kaepernick threw for 233 yards on 16 of 21 passes for 1 touchdown and 0 interceptions. He had a 76.19 completion percentage. His counterpart, Matt Ryan threw for 396 yards on 30 of 42 passes for 3 touchdowns and 1 interception. Ryan's completion percentage was 71.43, which was 4.7 percent below Kaepernick.

Further raising worries about the 49ers' kicking game, David Akers missed the only field goal he attempted, although he did hit 4 of 4 extra points.

Vernon Davis had a great day, catching 5 passes for 106 yards and 1 touchdown. Also almost reaching 100 yards, Frank Gore ran for 90 yards and 2 touchdowns on 21 carries.

Total yards went to Atlanta (477-373), along with passing yards (396-224) and 1st downs (27-21). San Francisco won rushing yards (149-81), penalty yards (24-30), and turnovers (1-2). The biggest difference in the game was red zone efficiency in which the 49ers dominated, going 4 for 5, while the Falcons were only 1 for 3.

2012 – 2013 San Francisco 49ers 87

Team Leaders

Passing

Colin Kaepernick #7
233 Yards, 1 Touchdown, 0 Interceptions
(16/21, 76.19 Comp %)

Rushing

Frank Gore #21
90 Yards on 21 Carries
4.29 Yards per Carry
2 Rushing Touchdowns

LaMichael James #23
34 Yards on 5 Carries
6.80 Yards per Carry
1 Rushing Touchdown

Colin Kaepernick #7
21 Yards on 2 Carries
10.50 Yards per Carry
0 Rushing Touchdowns

Receiving

Vernon Davis #85
106 Yards on 5 Receptions
21.20 Yards per Reception
1 Touchdown Reception

Michael Crabtree #15
57 Yards on 6 Receptions
9.50 Yards per Reception
0 Touchdown Receptions

Randy Moss #84
46 Yards on 3 Receptions
15.33 Yards per Reception
0 Touchdown Receptions

Delanie Walker #46
20 Yards on 1 Reception
20.00 Yards per Reception
0 Touchdown Receptions

Kicking

David Akers #2
4 Points Total
0/1 Field Goals
4/4 Extra Points

Interceptions

Chris Culliver #29
1 Interception

2012 – 2013 SAN FRANCISCO 49ERS 89

THE BOTTOM LINE

13 - 4 - 1

NFC CHAMPIONS

DAN FATHOW 90

PART II:
SUPER BOWL XLVII
THE MATCHUP VS. THE RAVENS

Dan Fathow 92

At the time Alex Smith was sidelined with his concussion injury in the second quarter of the game against the St. Louis Rams in Week 10, the 49ers were 6-2, and he led the entire NFL with a 70.18 percent completion percentage (153 of 218). He had 13 touchdowns with only 5 interceptions, meaning he threw 2.6 touchdowns for every interception. He also had a passer rating of 104.1. In addition, Smith had a nearly perfect game in Week 8 against the Cardinals, connecting on 18 of 19 passes, and he was nearly perfect in the game he was injured, having connected on 7 of 8 passes for 1 touchdown with 0 interceptions. In Hollywood-movie-fashion, Alex Smith's last pass before coming out of the game was a 14-yard touchdown pass.

This athlete became injured and was not allowed an opportunity to return to his position when he had recovered. With all of the concussion-related lawsuits pending against the NFL, it was very surprising that the league did not get involved in this situation or at least reprimand Jim Harbaugh.

Why should the league care if a quarterback is not allowed to compete for his position after suffering a concussion?

The reason is obvious. If a quarterback, who has done so much for his team as Smith had in 2012, is not allowed a chance to return to his position following a concussion, the message is that a quarterback with a concussion may be unfairly replaced. The result of that message is that quarterbacks and other athletes will realize they may have a lot to gain by hiding an injury, especially a concussion. Continuing to play with a concussion greatly increases permanent injury. These permanent injuries have resulted in the numerous lawsuits of which the NFL is currently terrified.

Other sports analysts have weighed in on the situation.

"No player should stay in the game with a concussion. Harbaugh inadvertently sent a really bad message across the NFL, and into every locker room: Even in this highly sensitive time when the league is trying to fight off lawsuits claiming players were not given the proper information about the dangers of concussions, he benched a player even after he was cleared by team doctors."
(Gary Meyers, *NY Daily News*, December 12, 2012:
http://www.nydailynews.com/sports/football/sunday-morning-qb-telling-truth-benched-article-1.1211546#ixzz2J738iOss)

Meyers makes an excellent point in that, as a former pro quarterback and a current head coach during the concussion crisis facing the NFL, Jim Harbaugh should know better than this. If he truly thought Kaepernick was the better quarterback, than that decision should be based on something – stats in games or clearly beating out Smith in practice. In fact, if he truly thought that, it would have happened *before* Smith was injured. A head coach may take any reason to replace a quarterback, but it had better be a good one or it could cost him his job. However, other possible reasons may have been valid *before* Smith was injured. While Smith was not playing, his stats couldn't change. He was just as good when he went out as when he was cleared to play. Nothing changed at all. If nothing changed, the only logical reason for replacing him is that the head coach thinks the player is less than he was before, meaning that he thinks the quarterback is damaged goods because of the concussion, despite the player being cleared by doctors to play. This is where this decision gets nasty and heated. The end result of this is undeniable: a quarterback has a lot to gain by hiding a concussion, which, supposedly, is the last thing the NFL wants a quarterback or any other player to do. The gains in hiding the injury are only professional and not medical, and as we all now dedicated athletes often sacrifice their bodies to achieve their goals, which for some leads to a debilitated future and regret. Putting this kind of pressure to hide injuries on quarterbacks is deplorable, even if it was unintentional.

Once again, if Smith came back and wasn't putting up the same numbers or winning as many games, then his replacement would be based on performance and not injury. If he is replaced without being allowed to play, his removal can only be based on the injury. Smith lost his job because of injury. Period.

By the numbers, the Smith-Kaepernick controversy came down to rushing abilities, because Kaepernick's numbers as a passing quarterback were not up to Smith's level. Kaepernick had a 98.3 passer rating. He put up 10 passing touchdowns, but at the expense of 3 interceptions and 9 fumbles. His completion percentage was 62.4. As said before, but it's very worth mentioning again: Smith led not only Kaepernick but the entire league with a 70.18 completion percentage, which was nearly 8 points higher than his replacement. Smith's passer rating was 104.1, nearly 6 points above Kaepernick. Smith only had 4 fumbles on the year, while Kaepernick had more than double that at 9 fumbles in fewer games.

Passing game aside, one cannot deny the remarkable, record-setting, rushing numbers that Colin Kaepernick put up in the post season. He certainly is a talented rusher, and he can throw off a defense because they don't know when he'll run on them, including all the way into the end zone. Kaepernick poses a unique threat that is hard to prepare for on defense. This discussion is not about Kaepernick's overall abilities, especially his post season rushing performances. This conversation is about documenting that there was nothing in Kaepernick's passing performances to put him above Smith as a starter.

The logical and controversial edge was obviously in Kaepernick's ground abilities. The argument over whether a quarterback should run so often is a heated one. While the quarterback is young and healthy, especially when he is breaking records as in the case of Kaepernick, it's hard to argue with letting him run and win games against strong opponents. The obvious downside is if he gets hurt, the team would be without their starting quarterback, who is the most prepared to play. If Kaepernick were to get injured in a way where he'd have to sit out for a half a season or more, especially if he never returned in condition to continue running the ball so often, the team would be at a loss, basically having risked too much injury to a quarterback, an injury that some would argue was inevitable and only a matter of time.

An example of the above conundrum would be the mess that the Washington Redskins found themselves in when Robert Griffin III was injured. As stated above, many would argue that he should not have been running so much because it made the injury inevitable. However, while he was rushing all over opponents, the critics weren't so loud. As with most coaching decisions, if you pull it off, you're the smartest mind in all of football, and if the gamble doesn't pay off, you're the stupidest coach in the history of the game. In this case RG3's passing stats were amazing for a first-year pro. 3,200 passing yards and a passing rating of 102.4 with 20 touchdowns and only 5 interceptions is an amazing rookie year. It's not too hard to argue that the best thing for Mr. Griffin and the Redskins would be to run Griffin less when he returns to play.

This applies to Kaepernick. While Kaepernick doesn't have the passing numbers as Griffin, his numbers are certainly good for a new starter, and they could definitely improve with more play, especially with more snaps resulting in pass attempts. As said above, it's an injury gamble. If Kaepernick stays healthy for years, Harbaugh will be considered a genius. However, if Kaerpenick gets injured with Smith already moved onto another team, the coach will receive the intense scorn of fans.

Yes, running backs obviously face this danger every game, but the average running back's career is much shorter than that of the average QB as a result of this danger. In addition, while running backs make great contributions to the game, entire offenses are not often built around them, as is often done for quarterbacks. As such, in most cases, the injury is much more devastating to the team's record when it is the quarterback who goes out.

It's a hard argument in which to draw a clear conclusion. Even if the 49ers win the Super Bowl with Colin Kaepernick, who is to say that they also would not have won with Alex

Smith, if he were given the same chance? And on the other hand, if the 49ers should lose to the Ravens, people may be quick to blame Kaepernick's performance and Harbaugh for playing him. But, who's to say that Alex Smith would have won the same game if given the opportunity?

    Because the same game, with the uncountable variables that go into it, can never be played twice, this is a controversy that will likely never be solved conclusively, and it certainly won't be solved by the outcome of the Super Bowl. One can only hope that Alex Smith has success with a new team in the future and that the 49ers will prosper with Kaepernick in the Super Bowl and beyond.

The Super Bowl XLVII Matchup

In the regular season, the Baltimore Ravens were 10-6, and the San Francisco 49ers were 11-4-1. Here are some key stats on how they both battled their way to the big game, side-by-side for a direct comparison.

TEAM	Points Scored	Points Allowed
Ravens	398	344
49ers	397	273

Team Passing Statistics

TEAM	Comp	Attempts	Comp %	Yards	TDs	Inter-Ceptions
Ravens	334	560	59.64%	3739	22	11
49ers	289	436	66.28%	3298	23	8

At first glance it would appear that the Ravens with 11 interceptions are throwing more passes away than the 49ers; however, there is more to it than that. The Ravens had 124 more pass attempts and 45 more completions than the 49ers. For every 54.5 pass attempts, the 49ers had 1 interception. For every 50.9 pass attempts, the Ravens threw 1 interception. There is not likely to be 50 pass attempts by either team, so it's hard to say who will throw more interceptions. The pressure of playing in the big game is likely to be a bigger factor in throwing an interception than regular season statistics. The other variable that is throwing some of the figures off is that nearly 8 games of the 49ers statistics were based on Alex Smith's performance and not Colin Kaepernick's.

In passing yards, the Ravens have the upper hand with having thrown 441 more yards than the 49ers. However, if you divide that by 16 games, the difference is 27.56 more passing yards per game, which is not that much of a difference or an advantage.

The 49ers have a higher completion ratio, but once again, that stat is colored with Alex Smith's figures. Kaepernick's regular season completion percentage is a bit lower at 62.4%, but that is still 2.76% higher than the Ravens' average. All in all, the passing numbers are fairly close for both teams.

TEAM RUSHING STATISTICS

TEAM	Carries	Yards	Average	Touchdowns
Ravens	444	1901	4.28 Yards	17
49ers	492	2491	5.06 Yards	17

The rushing numbers are also not too far apart. The 49ers rushed for more yards, with a higher average of 5.06 yards per carry, which is 0.78 yards more per carry than the Ravens. While 0.78 of a yard more per carry may not seem like much, it is 28.08 inches more or 2 feet 4 inches more per carry than the Ravens. When first downs and even touchdowns often come down to inches, this may or may not be a factor in this contest.

Both teams rushed for 17 touchdowns, so they have about equal ability to run the ball in to the end zone.

TEAM KICKING STATISTICS

TEAM	Extra Points	Extra Point %	Field Goals Made	Field Goals Attempted	Field Goal %	Total Points
Ravens	42	100%	30	33	90.90%	132
49ers	44	100%	29	42	69.04%	131

A cursory glance at points made might lead one to believe the kicking game is about even, but the Baltimore Ravens have a decisive advantage in the kicking game. The key is the field goal percentage. While the Ravens hit 30 field goals for 90 points and the 49ers hit 29 field goals for 87 points, Baltimore did it on 33 attempts, while it took the 49ers 42 attempts. So, that's 9 more attempts to kick 1 less field goal. Statistically, the Ravens are hitting 91% of their field goals, while the 49ers are only hitting 69% of their field goals. That is a significant difference that could easily affect the outcome of this game.

TEAM DEFENSIVE TURNOVERS

TEAM	Interceptions	Fumbles
Ravens	13	12
49ers	14	11

The defensive turnovers are very close. The Ravens have one more interception, while the 49ers have one more fumble resulting in a turnover. The ability of each team to force turnovers is nearly identical.

Quarterback Matchup
Flacco vs. Kaepernick

By the numbers:

Joe Flacco
Career Stats

Year	CMP	ATT	YDS	CMP%	TD	INT
2012	317	531	3,817	59.70	22	10
2011	312	542	3,610	57.56	20	12
2010	306	489	3,622	62.58	25	10
2009	315	499	3,613	63.13	21	12
2008	257	428	2,971	60.05	14	12

2012 Stats Chart
Regular Season - Post – Career

	CMP	ATT	YDS	CMP %	Avg	TD	INT
2012 Regular Season	317	531	3,817	59.70	7.19	22	10

2012 Postseason	51	93	853	54.84	9.17	8	0
Career	1,507	2,489	17,633	60.54	7.08	102	56

COLIN KAEPERNICK
CAREER STATS

Year	CMP	ATT	YDS	CMP%	TD	INT
2012	136	218	1,814	62.39	10	3
2011	3	5	35	60.00	0	0

2012 STATS CHART
REGULAR SEASON - POST — CAREER

	CMP	ATT	YDS	CMP%	AVG	TD	INT
2012 Regular Season	136	218	1,814	62.39	8.32	10	3
2012 Postseason	33	52	496	63.46	9.54	3	1
Career	139	223	1,849	62.33	8.29	10	3

The experience factor hands down goes to Joe Flacco, who has been in the league for 5 years, holding a record for winning at least 1 playoff game in all 5 years of his pro career.

While many have focused on Kaepernick's explosive record-setting running performance in the post season, Flacco has better numbers as a passing quarterback. Flacco has passed for 8 touchdowns with 0 interceptions in the post season, while Kaepernick has only passed for 3 touchdowns with 1 interception. Flacco also threw for nearly double the yards as Kaepernick, 853-496 (1.72 times as many yards as his opponent). However, Kaepernick has a better completion percentage, albeit on fewer passes, of 63.46% to Flacco's 54.84%.

Without Kaepernick's running game, Flacco would clearly be the most effective quarterback in the 2013 post season. But if Kaepernick rushes anywhere in the ballpark of the amazing 181 yards that he put up against Green Bay, it will be very hard for the Ravens to compete, barring a lot of failed 3rd and 4th down conversions and/or turnovers. The obvious other side of the coin is that if the Ravens shut down Kaepernick's rushing game, Flacco should be able to lead his team to victory. That's where the Kaepernick-Smith controversy really hits home for 49ers fans. If Kaepernick can run effectively in the Super Bowl, the decision will prove to have been a genius one.

CHECK OUT MORE GREAT RELEASES FROM
MEGALODON ENTERTAINMENT LLC

THE NEW ORLEANS SAINTS STORY
THE 43-YEAR ROAD TO THE SUPER BOWL XLIV CHAMPIONSHIP

Dan Fathow

Follow the **New Orleans Saints** through their amazing **Super Bowl XLIV (44) Championship** season, and re-experience every game, relive every score, and savor every victory. Travel with The Saints on their long, often trying 43 years on the road to success. Compare the stats on every Saints Quarterback. Who has the most yards, wins, and completions? Archie Manning, Drew Brees, Bobby Hebert, or Aaron Brooks? Find out which Saints coach has the best record and the most games. Sean Payton, Jim Mora, or Bum Phillips? This book is the perfect companion for new and long-time Saints fans alike.

ISBN 978-0-9800605-7-7

ALSO BY DAN FATHOW
THE 2012-2013 ALABAMA CRIMSON TIDE

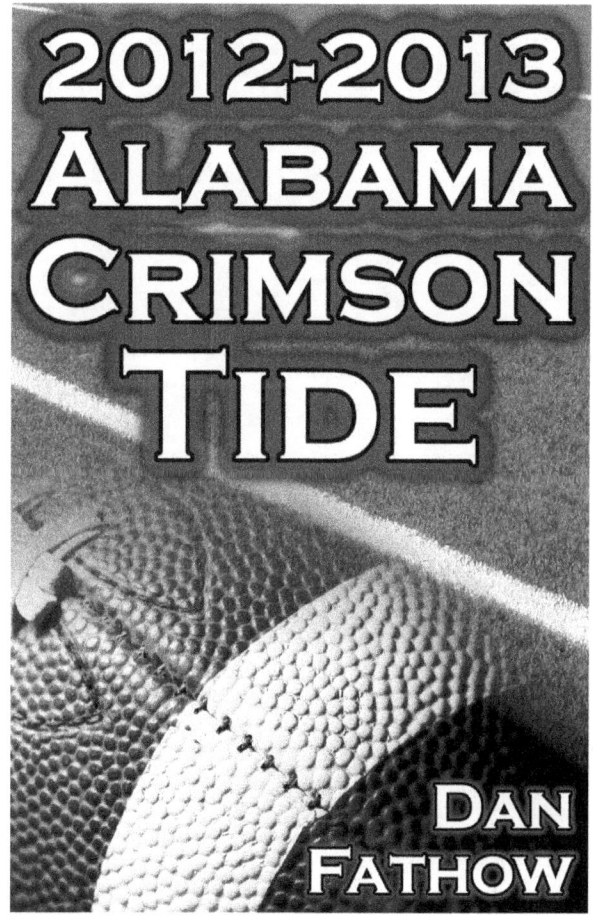

The defending BCS national champions, the 2012 Alabama Crimson Tide, dominated opponents throughout the season, earning a repeat trip to the 2013 BCS National Championship Game. Quarterback A.J. McCarron had a stellar year, putting up great numbers and leading his team back to the big game. Legendary coach Nick Saban kept his team focused and playing sharp, smart football all year long, becoming SEC Champions along the way. Follow the Crimson Tide as they destroy opponents, including their rival LSU Tigers and the Georgia Bulldogs in two of the most exciting and most talked about games of the year. Relive the magical 2012 season, victory by victory, quarter by quarter, and score by score all the way to the 2013 BCS National Championship Game against the Notre Dame Fighting Irish.

ISBN: 978-1-61589-038-5

www.ingramcontent.com/pod-product-compliance
Lightning Source LLC
Chambersburg PA
CBHW070512090426
42735CB00012B/2746